YOU'RE KIDDING!

Incredible Facts about the

PRESIDENTS

by Elizabeth Koehler-Pentacoff

illustrated by Donna Reynolds

For Paula

INTRODUCTION

Can you recite the names of all the American presidents—in order? Don't worry, not many people can. But if you discover funny or interesting details about their lives, you might be able to remember the presidents more easily.

This book is packed with facts about each president (did you know that three of our presidents died on the Fourth of July?). You'll also find anecdotes about some first ladies, tidbits about some first pets (including an alligator and a hyena), and little-known facts about some of the vice presidents. After you've finished reading, see how much you remember by taking the quiz on page 62.

1. GEORGE WASHINGTON

NICKNAME: FATHER OF HIS COUNTRY
PARTY: FEDERALIST
BORN: FEBRUARY 22, 1732
DIED: DECEMBER 14, 1799
TERM OF OFFICE: 1789–1797

PRESIDENTIAL HIGHLIGHTS:
BILL OF RIGHTS ENACTED;
POSTAL SYSTEM ESTABLISHED

BET YOU DIDN'T KNOW

☆ George liked to throw parties, but they ended at 9 P.M. (Martha's—his wife's—bedtime).

☆ Toothless by age fifty-seven, he had false teeth made out of walrus tusks and cow teeth! (*Not* wood.)

☆ He was the first president whose likeness appeared on a U.S. postage stamp (issued in 1847).

☆ He was the only president not to live in Washington, D.C.

☆ When he was reelected in 1793, George gave the shortest inauguration speech on record—133 words.

☆ He had to borrow money in 1789 to travel to New York for his inauguration.

☆ There's no proof that *George* ever chopped down a cherry tree, but he *was* a fabulous farmer.

☆ He wasn't *really* our country's first president. John Hanlon was president of the Thirteen States in the Confederation.

2. JOHN ADAMS

NICKNAME: HIS ROUNDNESS!
PARTY: FEDERALIST
BORN: OCTOBER 30, 1735
DIED: JULY 4, 1826
TERM OF OFFICE: 1797–1801

PRESIDENTIAL HIGHLIGHTS:

MISSISSIPPI TERRITORY CREATED; NAVY AND MARINE CORPS BEGAN;
LIBRARY OF CONGRESS ESTABLISHED

BET YOU DIDN'T KNOW

☆ He was the first president to live in the White House. His wife, Abigail, dried the laundry in the East Room.

☆ After they moved to Washington, D.C., John and Abigail explored the nearby forest. They were lost for two hours!

☆ Adams was our longest-living president. He died when he was 91.

☆ He suffered from mood swings.

☆ At 5 feet 7 inches (1.7 m) Adams weighed a hefty 250 pounds (113 kg).

☆ Adams was vice president for eight years and president for four.

☆ He won the presidency by only three electoral votes. Runner-up Thomas Jefferson became vice president.

☆ John Adams died on July 4, 1826. His last words were, "Thomas Jefferson still survives." (He didn't know that Jefferson had died earlier that day!)

3. THOMAS JEFFERSON

NICKNAME: FATHER OF THE
DECLARATION OF INDEPENDENCE
PARTY: DEMOCRAT-REPUBLICAN
BORN: APRIL 13, 1743
DIED: JULY 4, 1826
TERM OF OFFICE: 1801–1809

PRESIDENTIAL HIGHLIGHTS: LOUISIANA PURCHASE

BET YOU DIDN'T KNOW

☆ Considered one of the greatest presidents, Jefferson was absentminded. He once suggested that elections be held yearly—every February 29th!

☆ When he bought the Louisiana Purchase, he acted without constitutional authority. Many Federalists were so angry, they wanted to secede from the Union.

☆ He began the practice of shaking hands rather than bowing.

☆ Author of the Declaration of Independence, he wrote it without referring to notes or books.

☆ He hated formality and fancy clothes. He often wore an old coat and slippers when he met with dignitaries!

☆ An inventor, he created the swivel chair, a letter-copying machine, and a pedometer.

☆ Jefferson designed his home, which he named Monticello. At age seventy-nine, he drew plans for the University of Virginia.

☆ He kept grizzly bears on the White House grounds. They were brought back from the Lewis and Clark expedition.

4. James Madison

Nickname: Father of the Constitution
Party: Democrat-Republican
Born: March 16, 1751
Died: June 28, 1836
Term of Office: 1809–1817

PRESIDENTIAL HIGHLIGHTS:
War of 1812

BET YOU DIDN'T KNOW

☆ Madison was our shortest president—5 feet 4 inches (1.6 m). He weighed a mere 100 pounds (45 kg).

☆ He was good friends with Thomas Jefferson. Before they were presidents, they were arrested in Vermont for taking a carriage ride in the countryside—on a Sunday!

☆ Madison was the first president to wear trousers. The earlier ones had worn knee breeches.

☆ In 1826, Madison became president of the University of Virginia.

☆ James and Dolley Madison reared Dolley's son from her first marriage. The young man had a drinking and gambling problem, and Madison went into debt paying off the boy's bills.

☆ Madison died in 1836 at the age of eighty-five, the last of the founding fathers.

5. JAMES MONROE

NICKNAME: ERA OF GOOD FEELING
(REFERRING TO THE ADMINISTRATION)
PARTY: DEMOCRAT-REPUBLICAN
BORN: APRIL 28, 1758
DIED: JULY 4, 1831
TERM OF OFFICE: 1817–1825

PRESIDENTIAL HIGHLIGHTS:
MONROE DOCTRINE

BET YOU DIDN'T KNOW

☆ Monrovia—the capital of the African country Liberia—was named after him.

☆ He couldn't be inaugurated in the House of Representatives' chambers. House Speaker Henry Clay wouldn't let him because they'd had an argument!

☆ Although fashions had changed, Monroe still wore knee breeches and buckled shoes.

☆ In contrast to Dolley Madison, who was friendly and popular, Elizabeth Monroe was withdrawn. Daughter, Eliza, attended to her mother's social visits outside the White House. Many historians think Elizabeth may have had epilepsy, and her embarrassment kept her a recluse.

☆ Monroe was the first president to travel on a steamship. That vessel later became the first American steamship to cross the Atlantic.

☆ He was the third president to die on the Fourth of July. He died five years after Adams and Jefferson.

6. JOHN QUINCY ADAMS

NICKNAME: OLD MAN ELOQUENT
PARTY: DEMOCRAT-REPUBLICAN
BORN: JULY 11, 1767
DIED: FEBRUARY 23, 1848
TERM OF OFFICE: 1825–1829

PRESIDENTIAL HIGHLIGHTS:
TARIFF OF ABOMINATIONS

BET YOU DIDN'T KNOW

☆ He walked four miles (6.4 km) each day at dawn to the Potomac. When the weather was warm, he'd remove his clothes and skinny-dip! A reporter once saw him in the river and sat on his clothes. She refused to leave until he gave her an interview!

☆ His ghost supposedly haunts the White House. He's said to be writing a speech against the Mexican War. He died before he could finish it.

☆ When Adams ran for president, neither he nor the other three candidates received a majority of the popular vote. One of Adams's opponents, Henry Clay, decided to withdraw from the election and back Adams, so Adams was declared the winner. Later, Clay became his secretary of state. Many people thought this appointment was unethical, and Adams was not reelected for a second term.

☆ Adams was the first president to be photographed.

7. ANDREW JACKSON

NICKNAME: OLD HICKORY
PARTY: REPUBLICAN, THEN DEMOCRAT
BORN: MARCH 15, 1767
DIED: JUNE 8, 1845
TERM OF OFFICE: 1829–1837

PRESIDENTIAL HIGHLIGHTS:
TEXAS WON INDEPENDENCE FROM MEXICO

BET YOU DIDN'T KNOW

☆ Jackson killed a man in a duel over the honor of his wife, Rachel. From this fight, he carried a bullet near his heart for the rest of his life.

☆ After his inauguration, fans mobbed him at a wild White House party. They climbed through windows to get a chance to shake his hand! Jackson escaped and spent the night at a hotel.

☆ His enemies called him "King Jackson" because he spent so much money spiffing up the White House with fancy chandeliers and furniture.

☆ Jackson was the first president to have an assassination attempt made against him. Fortunately, the would-be murderer's pistols misfired.

☆ Jackson was thirteen when he was captured by the British during the Revolutionary War. An English officer cut him with a sword for refusing to clean his boots. He then made the wounded Jackson march 40 miles (64 km) to a military prison.

8. MARTIN VAN BUREN

NICKNAME: OLD KINDERHOOK
PARTY: DEMOCRAT
BORN: DECEMBER 5, 1782
DIED: JULY 24, 1862
TERM OF OFFICE: 1837–1841

PRESIDENTIAL HIGHLIGHTS:

TEN-HOUR WORK DAY ESTABLISHED FOR FEDERAL EMPLOYEES; FIRST
NAVAL EXPEDITION TO ANTARCTICA; TEMPORARY TREASURY NOTES
ISSUED DURING THE PANIC OF 1837

BET YOU DIDN'T KNOW

☆ His nickname—which was the result of his being born in Kinderhook, New York—got shortened to "O.K." This is thought to be the origin of this slang term.

☆ Van Buren began to study law when he was fourteen. He took part in his first court trial at the age of fifteen.

☆ His opponents called him "Martin Van Ruin" and blamed the 1837 economic depression on him.

☆ Some called him "Petticoat Pet" since he dressed fashionably.

☆ Van Buren was the first president born an American citizen.

☆ He was considered the first real politician. He liked to please everyone. Once, he spoke for an hour on tariffs. After the speech, people didn't know if he was for or against tariffs!

9. WILLIAM HENRY HARRISON

NICKNAME: TIPPECANOE
PARTY: WHIG
BORN: FEBRUARY 9, 1773
DIED: APRIL 4, 1841
TERM OF OFFICE: 1841–1841 (31 DAYS!)

PRESIDENTIAL HIGHLIGHTS:
HE DIDN'T HAVE TIME TO HAVE ANY!

BET YOU DIDN'T KNOW

☆ He was the only president to have a grandson who became president (Benjamin Harrison).

☆ In 1811, he defeated the Shawnee Indians at the Tippecanoe River. His presidential campaign managers remembered his military career when they came up with the slogan "Tippecanoe and Tyler too." (John Tyler was running as vice president.)

☆ Harrison won the presidency in part by claiming Van Buren ate from golden spoons, while he was a common man who had been born in a log cabin. He, however, was actually born in a three-story brick mansion!

☆ Harrison made the longest inauguration speech on record— 8,443 words.

☆ He had the shortest presidential term to date—from March 4, 1841 to April 4, 1841. Harrison refused to wear a hat and coat in the freezing rain on inauguration day, and he rode a horse in the parade instead of riding in a carriage. After spending hours out in that horrible weather, he caught a cold. It turned into pneumonia, and he died a month later.

10. JOHN TYLER

NICKNAME: OLD VETO
PARTY: WHIG
BORN: MARCH 29, 1790
DIED: JANUARY 18, 1862
TERM OF OFFICE: 1841–1845

PRESIDENTIAL HIGHLIGHTS:

U.S./BRITAIN LAND TREATY; U.S./CHINA TRADE TREATY

BET YOU DIDN'T KNOW

☆ After his first wife, Letitia, died, he married Julia. He was the first president to marry while in office.

☆ He was thirty years older than his second wife.

☆ He had more children than any other president—fifteen! He was seventy when his last child was born.

☆ He was the first vice president to succeed to the office of president.

☆ Tyler was an unpopular president, and members of his own party tried to impeach him.

☆ In 1861, he was elected to the Confederate House of Representatives. When he died, Whig leaders wouldn't even announce his death—because he served under the Confederate Congress.

11. JAMES K. POLK

NICKNAME: YOUNG HICKORY
PARTY: DEMOCRAT
BORN: NOVEMBER 2, 1795
DIED: JUNE 15, 1849
TERM OF OFFICE: 1845–1849

PRESIDENTIAL HIGHLIGHTS:

UNITED STATES DECLARED WAR ON MEXICO; WESTERN TERRITORY CLAIMED FOR THE UNITED STATES; ELECTION DAY STANDARDIZED

BET YOU DIDN'T KNOW

☆ At age sixteen, he had a gallstone operation and refused any anesthesia.

☆ James and Sarah, his wife, didn't believe in drinking, dancing, or card playing. At the inaugural ball, the music stopped when they entered the room. After they left, the party continued.

☆ His wife was also his secretary. They worked twelve to fourteen hours each day.

☆ When he began his term, Polk drew up a list of four major objectives. He accomplished them all!

☆ Polk was the first president not to seek reelection.

☆ Some people claim we had a "one-day president." Polk's term ended at noon on Sunday, March 4, 1849, but the next president, Taylor, wasn't inaugurated until Monday, March 5. Polk's vice president, George M. Dallas, had already resigned as president of the Senate on March 2. So, technically, the president of the Senate pro-tempore, David Rice Atchison, was president of the United States for twenty-four hours.

12. Zachary Taylor

NICKNAME: OLD ROUGH AND READY
PARTY: WHIG
BORN: NOVEMBER 24, 1784
DIED: JULY 9, 1850
TERM OF OFFICE: 1849–1850

PRESIDENTIAL HIGHLIGHTS:
CLAY COMPROMISE

BET YOU DIDN'T KNOW

☆ He never voted in an election. He didn't even vote for himself!

☆ When the Whigs wrote to Taylor to ask him to be their candidate, he refused the letter. It came with ten cents postage due, and he didn't want to pay for it!

☆ Taylor was a sloppy dresser who chewed tobacco. His wife, Margaret, smoked a corncob pipe.

☆ Margaret prayed he wouldn't become president. She hated being first lady. She stayed in her room and let her twenty-five-year-old daughter, Betty, play hostess.

☆ On a hot July 4, 1850, Taylor attended a ceremony for the unfinished Washington Monument. After the event, he went home, drank cold milk, and ate lots of cherries. He got sick and died five days later.

13. Millard Fillmore

Nickname: The American Louis Philippe
Party: Whig
Born: January 7, 1800
Died: March 8, 1874
Term of Office: 1850–1853

Presidential Highlights:

Sent Commodore Perry to Japan to open world trade; Passed the Compromise of 1850 to prevent civil war; Started the White House library

Bet you didn't know

☆ Fillmore could barely read at twenty, but he bought a dictionary and studied in every free moment he had. By the time he was thirty, he had worked as a teacher and a lawyer.

☆ When he was nineteen years old, he fell in love with his teacher! They waited seven years to marry.

☆ Abigail was the first first lady to have earned her own living.

☆ Fillmore was the first president to have a stepmother.

☆ Fillmore was a bibliophile. He owned four thousand books. When he became president, the White House didn't have any books. Not even a Bible! So Abigail started a White House library.

☆ Fillmore was the first president to have his food cooked on a stove. He even taught the cook how to use the new appliance!

14. FRANKLIN PIERCE

NICKNAME: HANDSOME FRANK
PARTY: DEMOCRAT
BORN: NOVEMBER 23, 1804
DIED: OCTOBER 8, 1869
TERM OF OFFICE: 1853–1857

PRESIDENTIAL HIGHLIGHTS:
GADSDEN PURCHASE

BET YOU DIDN'T KNOW

☆ Pierce was the only president not to swear when he was inaugurated. He "affirmed."

☆ When his wife, Jane, discovered he was a presidential candidate, she fainted!

☆ Pierce was the first president to have a Christmas tree in the White House.

☆ History hints that Pierce had a drinking problem.

☆ He entered Bowdoin College at age fifteen. His classmates included Henry Wadsworth Longfellow and Nathaniel Hawthorne.

☆ He and Jane spent their honeymoon in a boarding house.

☆ Pierce was the first president to have a full-time bodyguard.

15. James Buchanan

Nickname: Old Buck
Party: Federalist, then Democrat
Born: April 23, 1791
Died: June 1, 1868
Term of Office: 1857–1861

Presidential Highlights:
Country moves toward civil war

Bet you didn't know

☆ He was the only president never to marry. When he was twenty-eight, his fiancée, Anne Coleman, died. Rumors spread that she killed herself after a misunderstanding with Buchanan.

☆ His niece, Harriet Lane, was his official hostess. She gave great parties and was very popular. A song called "Listen to the Mockingbird" was dedicated to her.

☆ Buchanan had a nervous twitch. He jerked his head.

☆ He was the first president to have a visit from the British royal family. Albert Edward, Prince of Wales, slept in Buchanan's bed, while the president slept on a couch in a hallway!

☆ Many people think he wasn't a good president because he allowed seven states to secede from the Union in the years leading up to the Civil War. He thought he'd make things worse by forcing them to remain in the Union.

☆ Buchanan was expelled from college for breaking the rules! He was eventually readmitted and earned excellent grades.

16. ABRAHAM LINCOLN

NICKNAME: HONEST ABE
PARTY: REPUBLICAN
BORN: FEBRUARY 12, 1809
DIED: APRIL 15, 1865
TERM OF OFFICE: 1861–1865

PRESIDENTIAL HIGHLIGHTS:

EMANCIPATION PROCLAMATION; CIVIL WAR

BET YOU DIDN'T KNOW

☆ He was the first president to be born outside of the original thirteen states (in Kentucky).

☆ He was the only president to receive a patent. His invention created air chambers that allowed ships to navigate shallow waters.

☆ The night before his inauguration, Lincoln wore a disguise of women's clothing to get into a hotel in Washington!

☆ Lincoln was the first president to let his beard grow. In 1860, a little girl wrote to him saying he should grow whiskers because his face was too thin. She also thought the ladies would like him more with long whiskers! He took her advice.

☆ He was the first president to have a child die while he was in office. Willie died from typhoid when he was eleven. Lincoln's wife, Mary, held seances and claimed Willie's ghost visited her regularly.

☆ Lincoln was assassinated five days after the Civil War ended. He and Mary had gone to Ford's Theater to see *Our American Cousin*. Actor John Wilkes Booth shot him, and he died the next day.

17. Andrew Johnson

Nickname: None
Party: Democrat
Born: December 29, 1808
Died: July 31, 1875
Term of Office: 1865–1869

Presidential Highlights:

United States bought Alaska; Fourteenth Constitutional Amendment ratified

Bet you didn't know

☆ Johnson's family was so poor he had to work instead of going to school. His wife taught him how to write and do arithmetic.

☆ Eliza, the first lady, was the youngest bride to marry a future president. She was sixteen when she married Andrew Johnson.

☆ He was the first president to have impeachment proceedings brought against him. When Johnson fired the secretary of war without permission from Congress, they voted to impeach him. The Senate, however, was one vote short of the two-thirds majority needed, and Johnson finished his term.

☆ When the U.S. government bought Alaska from Russia, some people thought it was a ridiculous purchase. They called it "Andy Johnson's Polar Bear Garden." (It cost less than two cents an acre!)

☆ He won a Senate seat after his presidential term ended.

☆ Johnson signed the Fourteenth Amendment into law, which made former slaves citizens of the U.S. and guaranteed them basic civil rights.

18. ULYSSES S. GRANT

NICKNAME: HERO OF APPOMATTOX
PARTY: REPUBLICAN
BORN: APRIL 27, 1822
DIED: JULY 23, 1885
TERM OF OFFICE: 1869–1877

PRESIDENTIAL HIGHLIGHTS:

YELLOWSTONE NATIONAL PARK ESTABLISHED; FIRST TRANSCONTINENTAL RAILROAD SERVICE

BET YOU DIDN'T KNOW

☆ Grant smoked twenty cigars a day. When newspapers reported his fondness for cigars, he received ten thousand boxes from fans.

☆ He hated being nude and refused to get completely undressed—even to bathe!

☆ Grant was superstitious. He would never retrace his steps. If he had to return someplace, he'd use another path.

☆ This military general who killed many men never ate rare meat. He couldn't stand the sight of blood.

☆ While Grant was a Union general, one of his servants accidentally threw a bowl of water into a river. The bowl had held Grant's false teeth! He couldn't eat solid food until a dentist came and made new teeth for him.

☆ Dying from throat cancer, Grant was deeply in debt. To earn money, he wrote his autobiography, finishing it just days before he died. Mark Twain got it published. It was the first best-seller in its category.

19. RUTHERFORD B. HAYES

NICKNAME: DARK-HORSE PRESIDENT
PARTY: REPUBLICAN
BORN: OCTOBER 4, 1822
DIED: JANUARY 17, 1893
TERM OF OFFICE: 1877–1881

PRESIDENTIAL HIGHLIGHTS:
END OF RECONSTRUCTION

BET YOU DIDN'T KNOW

☆ Hayes was the first president to marry a college graduate.

☆ He didn't receive the popular vote, and the Electoral College votes looked questionable—so some people called the president "Rutherfraud."

☆ The president and his wife, Lucy, didn't drink or serve alcohol. Some people called the first lady "Lemonade Lucy."

☆ Hayes had long whiskers, which dipped into his soup! He moved them to the side before he ate.

☆ Hayes and his wife were outgoing. Sometimes they invited so many people to stay at the White House that their son, Webb, had to give up his room and sleep on the pool table in the attic!

☆ Lucy started the tradition of having an Easter egg roll on the White House lawn.

☆ Hayes was the first president to have a typewriter in his office.

20. JAMES A. GARFIELD

NICKNAME: NONE
PARTY: REPUBLICAN
BORN: NOVEMBER 19, 1831
DIED: SEPTEMBER 19, 1881
TERM OF OFFICE: 1881–1881

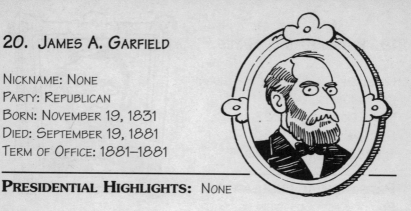

PRESIDENTIAL HIGHLIGHTS: NONE

BET YOU DIDN'T KNOW

☆ At sixteen, Garfield became a mule driver on a canal. He fell into the water more than a dozen times in six weeks!

☆ He taught Greek and Latin in college. One of his students was his future wife, Lucretia.

☆ Garfield wrote Greek with one hand and Latin with the other—at the same time!

☆ He was the last president born in a log cabin.

☆ When Charles Guiteau shot Garfield in the back, doctors couldn't get the bullet out. They even asked Alexander Graham Bell to help find the bullet with one of his inventions, but their efforts didn't work. Garfield lingered for eighty days but eventually died.

☆ While Garfield suffered, a heat wave hit the city. To take his mind off the heat, Lucretia and the president talked of old times and how they cut ice from a pond to store it for later use. That gave her an idea. She placed ice around his bed. Volunteers waved fans to help the cool air flow. Inventors created a device to hold the ice and trap moisture. This was the first "air-conditioning machine."

21. CHESTER A. ARTHUR

NICKNAME: GENTLEMAN BOSS
PARTY: REPUBLICAN
BORN: OCTOBER 5, 1829
DIED: NOVEMBER 18, 1886
TERM OF OFFICE: 1881–1885

PRESIDENTIAL HIGHLIGHTS:

CIVIL SERVICE COMMISSION ORGANIZED

BET YOU DIDN'T KNOW

☆ He wouldn't move into the White House until more than twenty wagonloads of old furniture and decorations were removed! He redecorated—with fringes and red velvet.

☆ A widower, he remained so romantic that he set a bouquet of flowers next to his dead wife's photograph every single day.

☆ He didn't want a bodyguard, but he was the first president to have a valet. His opponents teased him about this and said he couldn't even dress himself!

☆ A fashionable dresser, he had eighty pairs of pants and changed his outfit several times each day.

☆ He may not have been born in the United States! Some historians think he was born in Canada. (If so, he was ineligible for the presidency.)

22. AND 24. GROVER CLEVELAND

NICKNAME: UNCLE JUMBO
PARTY: DEMOCRAT
BORN: MARCH 18, 1837
DIED: JUNE 24, 1908
TERM OF OFFICE: 1885–1889
AND 1893–1897

PRESIDENTIAL HIGHLIGHTS:

PASSED FEDERAL BUSINESS CONTROLS; FINANCIAL PANIC OF 1893

BET YOU DIDN'T KNOW

☆ As a sheriff in 1870, Cleveland hanged two men!

☆ He paid someone $150 so he wouldn't have to fight in the Civil War. He stayed home to support his mother and sisters.

☆ His fiancée, Frances (Frankie), was twenty-one when she married her forty-nine-year-old guardian, "Uncle Cleve." He was the only president to be married in the White House. He wrote the invitations himself.

☆ He was the second-fattest president, weighing 260 pounds (117 kg). His opponents called him "Mr. Tubby."

☆ Cleveland had secret surgery while on a yacht. To treat a cancerous tumor in his jaw, his doctor cut out part of his upper jawbone. He wore a removable rubber device to make his face appear normal. Cleveland and government leaders thought the shaky economy would plunge if the American people knew their leader was ill. His doctor did not reveal the truth until 1917. The tumor is on display at a museum in Philadelphia!

☆ He was the only president elected to nonconsecutive terms.

23. Benjamin Harrison

NICKNAME: LITTLE BEN
PARTY: REPUBLICAN
BORN: AUGUST 20, 1833
DIED: MARCH 13, 1901
TERM OF OFFICE: 1889–1893

PRESIDENTIAL HIGHLIGHTS:
PAN-AMERICAN CONFERENCE; SHERMAN ANTITRUST ACT

BET YOU DIDN'T KNOW

☆ He was the only president to have a grandfather who was president.

☆ He was named for his great-grandfather, who signed the Declaration of Independence.

☆ An avid fisherman, Harrison spit on his worms for good luck!

☆ Carolyn, his wife, inspected the White House when they first moved in. The attic was filled with rats, and an armed assistant shot at any that came too close to her!

☆ Harrison was the last president to grow a beard.

☆ More states were admitted into the Union during this administration than in any other (South Dakota, North Dakota, Montana, Washington, Idaho, and Wyoming).

☆ Electricity was installed in the White House in 1891, but the president and first lady were afraid to touch the switches! They had servants turn the lights on and off.

☆ Harrison's presidency was the first to have full photographic coverage in newspapers and magazines.

25. William McKinley

NICKNAME: IDOL OF OHIO
PARTY: REPUBLICAN
BORN: JANUARY 29, 1843
DIED: SEPTEMBER 14, 1901
TERM OF OFFICE: 1897–1901

PRESIDENTIAL HIGHLIGHTS:

OPEN DOOR POLICY; SPANISH-AMERICAN WAR

BET YOU DIDN'T KNOW

☆ The first lady suffered from depression and epilepsy. She often sat next to the president at public events. When she had seizures, McKinley would place a napkin or handkerchief over her face until it was over.

☆ He was the first president to campaign using a telephone. He didn't travel and give speeches, like his opponent, William Jennings Bryan. McKinley didn't want to leave his wife's side.

☆ McKinley liked cigars but didn't want his picture taken smoking one. He didn't think it was a good example for children.

☆ He was the third president to be assassinated. While shaking hands with the public at the Pan American Exposition in Buffalo, New York, McKinley offered his hand to Leon Czolgosz. Czolgosz extended his covered right hand, in which he held a gun, and shot the president.

☆ He was the first president to ride in a self-propelled vehicle—an electric ambulance after he was shot. He died eight days later.

26. Theodore Roosevelt

NICKNAME: TR
PARTY: REPUBLICAN
BORN: OCTOBER 27, 1858
DIED: JANUARY 6, 1919
TERM OF OFFICE: 1901–1909

PRESIDENTIAL HIGHLIGHTS:

TRUST BUSTING; CONSTRUCTION OF
THE PANAMA CANAL BEGAN; UNITED STATES FOREST SERVICE ESTABLISHED

BET YOU DIDN'T KNOW

☆ Roosevelt was often ill with asthma when he was a child. He overcame this affliction by building up his physical strength.

☆ Before he became president, he was a cowboy and a rancher.

☆ He led a cavalry regiment, which became known as the Rough Riders, during the Spanish-American War.

☆ He was the youngest president (forty-two) to assume office.

☆ The six Roosevelt children and their friends had fun in the White House. They walked on stilts, had pillow fights, and roller skated in the East Room. Roosevelt allowed his children to bring their pets—even a pony and snakes!—indoors.

☆ Roosevelt was the first president to win the Nobel Peace Prize.

☆ Roosevelt was an avid sportsman. Once, while hunting, he found a bear cub but wouldn't shoot it. His compassion made the news, and a toy manufacturer began selling the "teddy" bear.

☆ He was the first president to invite an African-American to the White House (botanist Booker T. Washington).

27. WILLIAM TAFT

NICKNAME: NONE
PARTY: REPUBLICAN
BORN: SEPTEMBER 15, 1857
DIED: MARCH 8, 1930
TERM OF OFFICE: 1909–1913

PRESIDENTIAL HIGHLIGHTS:

SIXTEENTH CONSTITUTIONAL AMENDMENT (INCOME TAX LAW) RATIFIED

BET YOU DIDN'T KNOW

☆ Taft was our heaviest president, weighing more than 300 pounds (135 kg).

☆ He had a special bathtub installed in the White House. Four men could fit in it!

☆ He was the only president to later become Chief Justice of the Supreme Court.

☆ Taft was the first president to have an automobile at the White House. (He collected four.)

☆ First lady Helen loved the cherry trees in Japan. So three thousand were planted on the White House grounds.

☆ Taft was the first president to open a baseball season by throwing out the first ball.

☆ Their milk cow, Pauline Wayne, grazed on the White House lawn.

☆ Taft is one of only two presidents buried at Arlington National Cemetery. The other is John F. Kennedy.

28. Woodrow Wilson

NICKNAME: Schoolmaster in Politics
PARTY: Democrat
BORN: December 29, 1856
DIED: February 3, 1924
TERM OF OFFICE: 1913–1921

PRESIDENTIAL HIGHLIGHTS:

Nineteenth Constitutional Amendment ratified, allowing women to vote; United States declares war on Germany (1917); Armistice signed, ending World War I (1918)

BET YOU DIDN'T KNOW

☆ Wilson was the first president to have regular White House press conferences.

☆ He is the only president to have earned a Ph.D.

☆ He and his first wife, Ellen, exchanged 1,400 love letters during their marriage. Ellen died during Wilson's first term in office. Wilson remarried seven months later.

☆ His three daughters often joined White House tours pretending to be sightseers. They'd make loud and rude comments about the president's daughters!

☆ Wilson was awarded the Nobel Peace Prize in 1919 for his efforts toward creating the League of Nations.

☆ He was the first president to appoint a woman to a subcabinet post: Anne Abbott Adams, assistant attorney general.

☆ Wilson suffered from so much indigestion that he carried his own stomach pump with him.

29. WARREN G. HARDING

NICKNAME: NONE
PARTY: REPUBLICAN
BORN: NOVEMBER 2, 1865
DIED: AUGUST 2, 1923
TERM OF OFFICE: 1921–1923

PRESIDENTIAL HIGHLIGHTS:

TEAPOT DOME SCANDAL; WASHINGTON CONFERENCE FOR THE LIMITATION OF ARMAMENTS

BET YOU DIDN'T KNOW

☆ Harding was the first president to ride to his inauguration in an automobile.

☆ His dog, Laddie Boy, would entertain at cabinet meetings!

☆ He was the first president to make a speech over the radio.

☆ His presidential race was the first one in which women had the constitutional right to vote.

☆ His wife, Florence, often rewrote his speeches for him.

☆ Harding's administration was filled with scandals. Two members of his staff committed suicide, and the interior secretary resigned and later went to prison.

☆ Harding mysteriously died in San Francisco, while on a national speaking tour. Florence wouldn't allow an autopsy. Some people speculated that the first lady killed her husband.

☆ Florence burned the president's papers after he died.

☆ Later, she was alone in a room with Harding's doctor when *he* collapsed and died!

30. CALVIN COOLIDGE

NICKNAME: SILENT CAL
PARTY: REPUBLICAN
BORN: JULY 4, 1872
DIED: JANUARY 5, 1933
TERM OF OFFICE: 1923–1929

PRESIDENTIAL HIGHLIGHTS:
NATIONAL DEBT REDUCED BY $2 BILLION

BET YOU DIDN'T KNOW

☆ After President Harding died unexpectedly, Vice President Coolidge took the presidential oath in the middle of the night from his father, who was a notary public.

☆ He was the only president born on the Fourth of July.

☆ He installed a mechanical bucking horse in his bedroom, which he rode for exercise.

☆ Occasionally, he'd push all of the alarm buttons by his desk. Security officers, aides, and secretaries would rush into the room. He just wanted to make sure everything worked!

☆ Coolidge was a quiet man. Once, a reporter said to him, "I made a bet that I could get you to say more than two words." Coolidge replied, "You lose."

☆ Once, while he and his wife slept in a hotel with secret service men outside their door, a robber entered their room through a window. He was a college student who had run out of money. The Coolidges gave him a loan and sent him back out the window so he wouldn't get caught!

31. HERBERT HOOVER

NICKNAME: NONE
PARTY: REPUBLICAN
BORN: AUGUST 10, 1874
DIED: OCTOBER 20, 1964
TERM OF OFFICE: 1929–1933

PRESIDENTIAL HIGHLIGHTS:
STOCK MARKET CRASH; THE GREAT DEPRESSION

BET YOU DIDN'T KNOW

☆ The president and the first lady, Lou, spoke Chinese to each other if they didn't want anyone else to know what they were saying.

☆ They were both geologists and traveled the world doing mining surveys.

☆ Lou was president of the Girl Scouts of America. She spoke four languages and read six!

☆ Hoover gave his government salary to charity.

☆ He didn't want to see White House servants. When he came down the hall or into a room, servants had to hide in closets!

☆ During the Depression, some people were so poor that they had to live in shacks made of tar paper. These groups of shacks were called "Hoovervilles." Broken automobiles pulled by mules were "Hoover-Wagons."

32. Franklin Delano Roosevelt

Nickname: FDR
Party: Democrat
Born: January 30, 1882
Died: April 12, 1945
Term of Office: 1933–1945

Presidential Highlights:
The New Deal program; World War II; Social Security Act

Bet you didn't know

☆ Stricken with polio at thirty-nine, Roosevelt used crutches, braces, and a wheelchair for the rest of his life. Photographers and reporters followed a policy of "open secrecy." They tried to cut his wheelchair out of photos and didn't mention his disability in their articles.

☆ His hard-working wife, Eleanor, shook hands at receptions for him. Sometimes she shook 1,500 hands at one event. (Sometimes she attended several events in a day!)

☆ Eleanor and Franklin were fifth cousins. When they married, her Uncle Teddy (the twenty-sixth president) gave her away.

☆ Roosevelt was the first president to appear on television.

☆ He appointed the first female cabinet officer: Frances Perkins, secretary of labor.

☆ During World War II, the White House cooks had to stand in line with their stamp books to get food from the ration board, just like everyone else.

☆ Roosevelt was the only president to be elected for more than two terms.

33. Harry S. Truman

NICKNAME: MAN OF THE PEOPLE
PARTY: DEMOCRAT
BORN: MAY 8, 1884
DIED: DECEMBER 26, 1972
TERM OF OFFICE: 1945–1953

PRESIDENTIAL HIGHLIGHTS:

UNITED NATIONS FORMED; WORLD WAR II ENDED; MCCARTHY'S UN-AMERICAN ACTIVITIES COMMITTEE FORMED

BET YOU DIDN'T KNOW

☆ Truman and his wife, Bess, were childhood sweethearts. They met when he was six and she was five.

☆ Truman liked to say the word "manure" a lot.

☆ His opponents in the 1948 campaign said, "To err is Truman."

☆ Everyone thought his opponent, Thomas Dewey, would win the presidency. The *Chicago Tribune* even printed an early edition of the newspaper with the headline, "Dewey Defeats Truman!"

☆ Truman's middle initial, "S," doesn't stand for anything. His parents couldn't decide on his middle name.

☆ When the White House was remodeled during his term, the scrap building materials were sold as souvenirs.

☆ After his presidency, when Disneyland opened, Truman wouldn't ride on the Dumbo ride. Why? Because an elephant is the Republican Party's mascot!

34. Dwight D. Eisenhower

Nickname: Ike
Party: Republican
Born: October 14, 1890
Died: March 28, 1969
Term of Office: 1953–1961

Presidential Highlights:

Korean War ended; Aeronautics and Space Administration created

Bet you didn't know

☆ Eisenhower was the first president to appear on color television.

☆ Ike was known for his favorite hobby—playing golf. He also liked to watch movies and read Western novels.

☆ He liked to paint but couldn't draw. So he had someone draw pictures, and then he'd paint them. This is how paint-by-numbers got started.

☆ He was the first president to hit a hole in one.

☆ His grandson, David, later married Julie Nixon, whose father, Richard Nixon, was Eisenhower's vice president and our thirty-seventh president.

☆ His wife, Mamie, decorated the White House for every holiday, including Halloween and Saint Patrick's Day.

35. JOHN FITZGERALD KENNEDY

NICKNAME: JFK
PARTY: DEMOCRAT
BORN: MAY 29, 1917
DIED: NOVEMBER 22, 1963
TERM OF OFFICE: 1961–1963

PRESIDENTIAL HIGHLIGHTS:

TEST BAN TREATY; PEACE CORPS; MEDICARE

BET YOU DIDN'T KNOW

☆ JFK was the youngest *elected* president. He was forty-three when he was inaugurated. (Theodore Roosevelt was forty-two when he *assumed* the office of president after William McKinley was assassinated.)

☆ He was the only president to win a Pulitzer Prize. He authored *Profiles in Courage.*

☆ Kennedy was the first Roman Catholic president.

☆ His inauguration speech includes one of the most famous presidential quotes. Kennedy said, "Ask not what your country can do for you; ask what you can do for your country."

☆ While JFK was serving in the navy during World War II, a Japanese destroyer cut his torpedo boat in half. He saved a man by holding his life jacket strap in his teeth!

☆ First lady Jackie brought culture to the White House. She held concerts and performances for both adults and children. Using private contributions, Jackie redecorated the White House with antiques and valuable pieces of art.

36. LYNDON BAINES JOHNSON

NICKNAME: LBJ
PARTY: DEMOCRAT
BORN: AUGUST 27, 1908
DIED: JANUARY 22, 1973
TERM OF OFFICE: 1963–1969

PRESIDENTIAL HIGHLIGHTS:

CIVIL RIGHTS ACT OF 1964; VIETNAM WAR; WAR ON POVERTY

BET YOU DIDN'T KNOW

☆ LBJ was the only president sworn into office by a female judge.

☆ As a child he learned the alphabet at age two. He could read by the time he was four.

☆ To earn money, he shined shoes, picked cotton, and worked on road construction crews.

☆ Johnson graduated from high school at age fifteen.

☆ He was the first U.S. president to hold press conferences while walking. Reporters had to walk so fast during these "walkie talkies," they were out of breath!

☆ He proposed to his future wife on their first date. They married two months later.

☆ This president from Texas handed out ten-gallon hats to visitors.

☆ LBJ's initials were also his family's initials. His wife (Claudia) was nicknamed Lady Bird, and their daughters were named Lynda Bird and Luci Baines. Their dogs were Little Beagle and Little Beagle Junior!

37. Richard Milhous Nixon

Nickname: None
Party: Republican
Born: January 9, 1913
Died: April 22, 1994
Term of Office: 1969–1974

Presidential Highlights:

Vietnam cease-fire agreement; Presidential visit to China; Watergate Scandal

Bet you didn't know

☆ As a teenager, Nixon was a barker at an Arizona rodeo.

☆ As a law student, he once broke into the dean's office to see his class ranking.

☆ He was the youngest Republican senator (thirty-seven).

☆ He was the only person elected twice to the offices of vice president and president. (Nixon was elected vice president for two terms under Dwight D. Eisenhower.)

☆ Nixon was the only president to win an Emmy (for an album of a television interview).

☆ Sometimes he'd forget to introduce his wife, Pat, to people— leaving her standing with her hand outstretched.

☆ Sometimes when he needed to communicate with his wife, he'd send her a memo.

☆ Nixon was the second president to have impeachment proceedings brought against him, and he was the only president to resign from office.

38. GERALD FORD

NICKNAME: JERRY
PARTY: REPUBLICAN
BORN: JULY 14, 1913
DIED: —
TERM OF OFFICE: 1974–1977

PRESIDENTIAL HIGHLIGHTS:

PARDONED RICHARD NIXON; NELSON ROCKEFELLER SWORN IN AS VICE PRESIDENT; HELSINKI ACCORDS

BET YOU DIDN'T KNOW

☆ He was first named Leslie Lynch King, Jr., after his father. His parents divorced, and when his mother remarried to a man named Gerald Ford, she changed her son's name.

☆ He could write with both hands.

☆ He once co-owned a New York modeling agency and modeled sports clothes for *Look* and *Cosmopolitan* magazines.

☆ First lady Betty danced professionally with Martha Graham.

☆ He had a chance to play professional football with the Green Bay Packers and the Detroit Lions but turned them down to attend law school.

☆ He was the only vice president and president to assume office by appointment—he was not elected to either office.

☆ An athlete, the president enjoyed golf and skiing. But he was also clumsy. He tripped down airplane steps and fell on ski trails.

39. James Earl Carter

Nickname: Jimmy
Party: Democrat
Born: October 1, 1924
Died: —
Term of Office: 1977–1981

Presidential Highlights:
Camp David Accords; Hostages taken in Iran

Bet you didn't know

☆ His family ran a peanut farm. When he was about five, he sold boiled peanuts on the streets of Plains, Georgia.

☆ He learned to read at four, and when he was twelve he read *War and Peace* (one thousand pages!).

☆ Carter lost a senate race in Georgia, but investigators discovered dead people had voted for his opponent! After a recount to find the *honest* votes, Jimmy won.

☆ He was the sixth president named James. (Remember Garfield, Buchanan, Polk, Monroe, and Madison?)

☆ His mother, Lillian, joined the Peace Corps when she was seventy.

☆ Carter was the first president born in a hospital.

☆ Many people believe he's one of the smartest presidents the United States has ever had.

☆ After leaving the White House, Jimmy and his wife, Rosalynn, both became carpenters! They built homes for the poor through Habitat for Humanity.

40. RONALD REAGAN

NICKNAME: THE GREAT COMMUNICATOR
PARTY: REPUBLICAN
BORN: FEBRUARY 6, 1911
DIED: —
TERM OF OFFICE: 1981–1989

PRESIDENTIAL HIGHLIGHTS:

REAGANOMICS; IRAN CONTRA AFFAIR; FIRST WOMAN APPOINTED TO THE SUPREME COURT

BET YOU DIDN'T KNOW

☆ As a teenager, he worked as a lifeguard. He saved seventy-seven people's lives!

☆ Reagan was once a Democrat. He even campaigned for Truman.

☆ As a radio sportscaster, he described games as though he was there. But he wasn't! He actually read the plays from a tickertape and made up the details! Once, the tape died and he had to fake six minutes of a baseball game.

☆ He was the first president to have once been a movie and television star. In *Bedtime for Bonzo*, his costar was a chimpanzee! In *Hellcats of the Navy*, his costar was Nancy Davis—his future wife.

☆ Reagan was the oldest elected president (sixty-nine).

☆ At seventy-seven, he was the oldest to leave the office.

☆ Reagan loved jelly beans so much he kept a jar of them on his desk.

41. GEORGE BUSH

NICKNAME: NONE
PARTY: REPUBLICAN
BORN: JUNE 12, 1924
DIED: —
TERM OF OFFICE: 1989–1993

PRESIDENTIAL HIGHLIGHTS:
PERSIAN GULF WAR

BET YOU DIDN'T KNOW

☆ During World War II, Bush was the navy's youngest pilot. He flew fifty-eight combat missions and survived four crashes.

☆ While Bush was on a mission, his plane was shot down over the Pacific. He parachuted into the ocean and floated on an inflatable raft. After paddling with his hands for three hours, he was finally rescued by an American submarine.

☆ Bush was the first vice presidential candidate (running with Ronald Reagan) to run against a female vice presidential candidate, Geraldine Ferraro.

☆ Bush was the first vice president to be elected to the presidency since Martin Van Buren.

☆ He was the first president to use a personal computer.

☆ When he said publicly that he hated broccoli, angry representatives of the broccoli industry sent truckloads of it to the White House!

42. WILLIAM JEFFERSON CLINTON

NICKNAME: BILL
PARTY: DEMOCRAT
BORN: AUGUST 19, 1946
DIED: —
TERM OF OFFICE: 1993—

PRESIDENTIAL HIGHLIGHTS:

REDUCED FEDERAL BUDGET DEFICIT; NORTH AMERICAN FREE TRADE
AGREEMENT; WHITEWATER SCANDAL

BET YOU DIDN'T KNOW

☆ Bill's first job was as a greeter in his grandfather's store. His pay? Candy!

☆ His father's name was William Jefferson Blythe IV. He was killed in a car accident three months before Bill was born. As a teenager, he changed his name to William Clinton, after his stepfather.

☆ In high school, Bill played saxophone in six different bands.

☆ He met President John F. Kennedy in 1963. There's even a photo of them shaking hands.

☆ Bill and his wife, Hillary, met as law students at Yale. As a lawyer, Hillary was the first future first lady to earn three times more money than her politician husband.

☆ Bill Clinton and Al Gore were the youngest president/vice president team ever. Clinton was forty-five when he was elected; Gore, forty-four.

☆ Clinton was the first president to appear on MTV and the first president to have a web site.

First Ladies

Abigail Adams had strong opinions, and she wasn't afraid to share them with her husband. In 1776, as he worked on the Declaration of Independence, she wrote to him, "Remember the ladies."

Dolley Madison, nicknamed "Queen Dolley," was a popular first lady. She used snuff, began the custom of serving ice cream at the White House, and rescued George Washington's portrait when the British burned down the White House. Once, she spent $40 on an imported mirror. The Senate investigated. The investigation cost $2,000!

Louisa Adams, John Quincy Adams's wife, was the only first lady born outside the United States. She was born in England and met her future husband while he was in London on a diplomatic assignment.

Sarah Polk, a very religious woman, wouldn't attend the theater or play cards. She didn't allow alcohol in the White House. She lived forty-two years longer than her husband. In all those years, she never left her house except to attend church!

Mary Lincoln was a clothes-a-holic! At the

time of her husband's death, she owed $27,000 in shopping bills. She also had temper tantrums when she didn't get her way.

Julia Grant's eyes were crossed. As first lady, she invited maids and royalty to her parties.

Caroline Harrison was the first first lady to manage a project in the White House. She oversaw its renovation.

Frances Cleveland was only twenty-one when she wed Grover. Some people gossiped that he should have married her mother. When companies used the first lady's name to advertise their products without her permission, Congress passed a law forbidding it. "Frankie" was so well-liked, people joined Frankie fan clubs all across the country.

Edith Wilson took over for her husband when he suffered a stroke. She denied, however, that she made any political decisions. Nonetheless, many people called her "Mr. President." They referred to this time as the "Petticoat government."

Eleanor Roosevelt, our most active first lady, served hot dogs for dinner when England's King George was visiting!

Mamie Eisenhower wore pink clothes, slept in a pink bed, and even had a pink toilet seat! She loved to stay in bed until noon. Her hobbies were watching soap operas and playing Scrabble.

Jackie Kennedy used private donations to restore the White House. In 1962, fifty-six million viewers watched an hour-long television special, "A Tour of the White House with Mrs. John F. Kennedy." Through her unique beauty and intelligence, Jackie left a lasting impression worldwide.

Pat Nixon impressed her future husband, Richard, so much that he proposed to her the very day he met her.

Betty Ford started the Betty Ford Center to treat people who have drug and alcohol addictions.

Nancy Reagan spent $200,000 on White House china while her husband cut back on Welfare spending. But her anti-drug campaign, "Just Say No to Drugs," along with her sense of humor, helped save her public image.

Barbara Bush didn't worry about fashion, and she disliked controversy. She focused her attention on improving literacy rates nationwide.

Hillary Clinton had more than three hundred different hairstyles between 1992 and 1996. Her hair even had a web site! She was the first first lady to have a postgraduate degree.

Important Political "Firsts" for Women

Victoria Woodhull, a founder of a Wall Street brokerage firm, was the first female presidential candidate. She ran on the Equal Rights Party ticket of 1872.

Belva Lockwood ran against Grover Cleveland in 1884. She received 4,149 votes. None of them were from women—since women couldn't vote until 1920.

Margaret Chase Smith was the first woman to try for a presidential nomination in a major political party. (She ran against Republican Senator Barry Goldwater in 1964. He won.)

Shirley Chisholm was the first black American to attempt to get the Democratic party's nomination. (She ran against Senator George McGovern in 1972. He won.) She was also the first black woman elected to the House of Representatives.

Geraldine Ferraro was the first female candidate for vice president. She and Walter Mondale ran against Ronald Reagan and George Bush in 1984.

EERIE COINCIDENCES IN THE LIVES OF ABRAHAM LINCOLN AND JOHN F. KENNEDY

☆ Both of these presidents were very concerned with civil rights.

☆ Lincoln took office in 1860, Kennedy in 1960.

☆ Lincoln's secretary, whose name was Kennedy, advised him not to go to the theater—where he was later assassinated.

☆ Kennedy's secretary, whose name was Lincoln, advised him not to go to Dallas—where he was later assassinated.

☆ Mary Lincoln and Jackie Kennedy both had children who died while their husbands were serving as president.

☆ Both men were killed on a Friday.

☆ John Wilkes Booth shot Lincoln while he was sitting in a theater, and then Booth hid in a warehouse.

☆ Lee Harvey Oswald shot Kennedy from a warehouse, and then Oswald hid in a theater.

☆ Both assassins were killed before they could be tried in court.

☆ John Wilkes Booth was born in 1839. Lee Harvey Oswald was born in 1939.

☆ Both presidents were succeeded by men named Johnson.

☆ Both Johnsons were Democrats.

☆ Andrew Johnson was born in 1808. Lyndon B. Johnson was born in 1908.

☆ Neither Johnson served a second term.

☆ The names Lincoln and Kennedy each contain seven letters. "Andrew Johnson" and "Lyndon Johnson" each have thirteen letters. "John Wilkes Booth" and "Lee Harvey Oswald" each have a total of fifteen letters.

☆ One week before the assassinations of both Lincoln and Kennedy, they were in Monroe, Maryland.

George Washington gave his dogs funny names, like Sweetlips and Madame Moose. He made his grooms brush his horses' teeth!

Thomas Jefferson's mockingbird barked like a dog and purred like a cat. He'd sing along while Jefferson played the violin. The bird would sit on Jefferson's shoulder during political meetings.

John Quincy Adams kept an alligator in the East Room for several months. His wife's silkworms made silk used in many of her gowns.

When the British burned the White House during the War of 1812, **Dolley Madison** escaped with not only a painting of George Washington—but also her parrot.

During **Andrew Jackson's** funeral, his parrot, Pol, swore repeatedly—and had to be taken away from the ceremony!

Poor "Old Whitey." Visitors often yanked hair from the tail of **Zachary Taylor's** horse for souvenirs. After Taylor's death, the horse walked in the funeral procession, with his master's boots turned backward in the stirrups.

Millard Fillmore founded a chapter of the American Society for the Prevention of Cruelty to Animals—but he believed people should own slaves!

Abraham Lincoln's goat ran through the White House and sometimes rode in the president's carriage. When Lincoln's son, **Tad,** discovered that Jack, the White House turkey, was destined to become Thanksgiving dinner, he desperately pleaded Jack's case to his father. Lincoln reportedly drew up a document allowing Jack to live.

When **Andrew Johnson** found mice in the White House, he fed them flour and gave them fresh water!

Ulysses S. Grant suspected his staff of killing his son's dogs. One day, he announced that if another dog died, everyone would be fired. Coincidentally, the animals stayed healthy from that time on.

Benjamin Harrison gave a goat to his grandchildren. Old Whiskers, as the goat was called, pulled the three children in a cart—through the White House gates! The president chased after them.

William McKinley taught his parrot to sing "Yankee Doodle" and "America."

Theodore Roosevelt's menagerie consisted of a bear, a lizard, a pig, a hyena, snakes, and a flying squirrel. His pony, named Algonquin, rode up and down in the White House elevator. His daughter Alice had a snake whom she named Emily Spinach.

William Taft's cow, Pauline Wayne, was the last presidential cow.

Woodrow Wilson kept sheep to trim the White House lawn. Their wool was sold to raise money for the Red Cross.

The Smithsonian Museum in Washington has a statue of **Warren G. Harding's** Airedale, Laddie Boy. While at the White House, Laddie Boy had a birthday party with the neighborhood dogs.

Calvin Coolidge had a house built for a raccoon he named Rebecca. He even walked her on a leash.

Herbert Hoover's opossum became a school baseball team's mascot. **Lou Hoover** created an aviary at the end of one White House hallway.

One of the most famous presidential animals was Fala, **Franklin Delano Roosevelt's** Scottie. He went everywhere with his master. It was rumored the president sent a destroyer to the Aleutian Islands to pick up the little dog after he had been mistakenly left there during one of Roosevelt's trips. But it wasn't true, and FDR said Fala's feelings had been hurt by the gossip!

Nikita Khruschev gave Pushinka, daughter of one of the first Russian dogs in space, to **John F. Kennedy.** U.S. government agents checked the animal for electronic bugs.

Lyndon Baines Johnson got in trouble with animal lovers when he picked up his beagle by the ears. Him, as the beagle was known, was the first dog to attend a presidential inaugural parade. LBJ's daughter **Luci** found a mutt, Yuki, and wrote his biography. LBJ shook Yuki's paw at a meeting—before shaking hands with the people who were present!

As a vice presidential candidate, **Richard Nixon** made his "Checker's Speech," telling everyone he was going to accept a personal gift to the family. The gift was a black cocker spaniel named Checkers.

When **Gerald Ford** wanted people to leave his office, he gave a command to his golden retriever, Liberty, who had been trained to break up meetings.

George Bush's wife, Barbara, wrote *Millie's Book*—a best-seller about the life of their spaniel. Millie slept right in between the president and the first lady in their bed.

Photographers from the media stalked **Bill Clinton's** cat, Socks, so much that the president ordered members of the press to keep their distance from the animal. His dog, Buddy, seemed to enjoy the limelight.

VICE PRESIDENTS

John Adams (served with George Washington) didn't always wear his dentures, so he lisped.

Thomas Jefferson (served with John Adams) said the Declaration of Independence didn't get much editing because the signers met in a room near a horse stable. No one could stand the flies! When Adams and Jefferson ran against each other for president, it hurt their friendship. It was the only time in history a vice president ran against a president, and the *vice president* won.

Aaron Burr (served with Thomas Jefferson) committed murder while he was vice president! He killed Alexander Hamilton in a duel. Up to this time, the "runner up" in the presidential race (the person with the second-most votes) became the vice president. The Twelfth Amendment was added to the Constitution to allow the electoral college to name both a president and a vice president.

John Calhoun (served with John Quincy Adams) was the first vice president to resign. (He did so nine weeks before his term ended!)

George M. Dallas (served with James K. Polk) is famous in Texas, where a city is named after him.

William Rufus DeVane King (served with Franklin Pierce) is the only bachelor vice president and was once a roommate of James Buchanan.

John Breckinridge (served with James Buchanan) joined the Confederate army as a general and was charged with treason. In 1865, Jefferson Davis, president of the Confederacy, named Breckinridge his vice president. When Richmond—the Confederate capital—fell, Davis and Breckinridge escaped. While hiding out near the Florida Keys, they were attacked by pirates. They floated in a small boat without food for two days before reaching Cuba.

Hannibal Hamlin (served with Abraham Lincoln) was vice president during Lincoln's first term. **Andrew Johnson** was Lincoln's vice president for only six weeks. So the question, "Who was Lincoln's vice president?" is a tricky one.

After Lincoln was shot, some authorities suspected **Andrew Johnson**. He had turned down an invitation from Lincoln to attend the theater with him, and Booth, Lincoln's assassin, left a personal note for Johnson to make him look suspicious.

Schuyler Colfax (served with Ulysses S. Grant) said he hadn't accepted any bribes in the Credit Mobilier Scandal, but evidence showed he lied and committed perjury.

William Wheeler (served with Rutherford B. Hayes) really liked Hayes—although it was unusual for vice presidents and presidents to be "buddies." The two families often socialized in the evenings and sang songs around the piano.

Adlai Ewing Stevenson (served with Grover Cleveland) didn't even know that Cleveland was having secret jaw surgery, since Cleveland often ignored his vice president. Stevenson *never* knew the truth. He died in 1914, and the facts didn't become public until three years later.

Charles Fairbanks (served with Theodore Roosevelt) and the president couldn't stand each other. Even so, Alaska named a city after this vice president.

Charles Dawes (served with Calvin Coolidge) won a Nobel Peace Prize for the Dawes Plan, which was a program created for Germany to pay its debt for damages incurred during World War I.

John Nance Garner (served with Franklin D. Roosevelt) was rejected when he applied to Vanderbilt University. Later, when the school wanted to give him an honorary degree, *he* turned *them* down!

Alben William Barkley (served with Harry S. Truman), at seventy-one was the only vice president to get married while in office. He wrote love letters to his thirty-eight-year-old girlfriend during Senate meetings!

Lyndon Baines Johnson (served with John F. Kennedy) called Kennedy's advisers "Georgetown Jelly Beans." They nicknamed him "Uncle Cornpone."

Spiro T. Agnew (served with Richard Nixon) admitted he had accepted bribes and evaded paying income tax. He resigned from office and had to pay $10,000 in fines. Agnew also served probation. Later he claimed he was innocent.

Nelson Rockefeller (served with Gerald Ford) was a billionaire and our richest vice president.

James Danforth Quayle (served with George Bush) once visited a school's spelling bee and made an embarrassing mistake. As a twelve-year-old student wrote out the word "potato" on the blackboard, Quayle suggested he should add an "e" at the end. Reporters loved his error!

QUIZ

DO YOU KNOW . . .

1. Which president turned down offers from two pro football teams in order to go to law school? _____

2. Who was the only president born on the Fourth of July?

    _____

3. This first lady served hot dogs to the king of England.

    _____

4. Who wouldn't ride "Dumbo" at Disneyland?

    _____

5. He had a pet alligator in the White House.

    _____

6. This vice president killed a man in a duel.

    _____

7. Which president and his wife spoke Chinese?

    _____

8. Who was our movie-star president?

    _____

9. This president and his wife were fifth cousins.

    _____

10. Who was the first female candidate for vice president?

    _____

11. Name the president who appeared on MTV.

    _____

12. Which president appointed the first female cabinet officer?
_____

13. Alaska named a city after this vice president, who served under Theodore Roosevelt: _____

14. This president walked his raccoon on a leash:
_____

15. Which president handed out ten-gallon hats to visitors?
_____

16. Which president was the only one to resign from office?
_____

17. The "Checkers Speech" was about which president's dog?
_____

18. Which first lady started the White House Easter egg roll? _____

19. Who was the first black woman elected to the House of Representatives? _____

20. Which president wrote the Declaration of Independence?
_____

(Answers are below, but don't peek.)

ANSWERS

1. Gerald Ford 2. Calvin Coolidge 3. Eleanor Roosevelt 4. Harry S. Truman 5. John Quincy Adams 6. Aaron Burr 7. Herbert and Lou Hoover 8. Ronald Reagan 9. Franklin and Eleanor Roosevelt 10. Geraldine Ferraro 11. William Clinton 12. Franklin D. Roosevelt 13. Charles Fairbanks 14. Calvin Coolidge 15. Lyndon B. Johnson 16. Richard Nixon 17. Richard Nixon 18. Lucy Hayes 19. Shirley Chisholm 20. Thomas Jefferson